ZION WILLINGHAM

Precept Upon Precept

Are You Called To Teach?

Contents

Preface

Are you called, chosen, or simply curious? The manifest series of books will explore each five-fold ministry call from biblical times until now. Precept Upon Precept is the fourth title in the Manifest Series of books. We will discuss the call to teach the Word of God in its operation throughout the years. It's time to arise and manifest!

I

Part One

1

Introduction

Arise to
Manifest

You are the person emerging from an F5 tornado clutching your books. Your conversations about the bible are seasoned with wisdom and anchored tightly to the Word of God. You feel a strong call to impart to others the nuggets of information that you have ingested in the Word of God. Most importantly, God has told you that you are called to share the Word of God. If this is you, then you just might be called as a teacher.

The Journey Online website defined the process of biblical teaching as:

"Teaching is the process whereby qualified leaders in the church, guided by the Holy Spirit and using Scripture as their authority, creatively structure and manage formal and informal learning experiences in such a way that students are:

1. Led to discover what Scripture says, what it means, how it applies to their lives, and to respond appropriately to its message.
2. Guided in the formation and expression of godly character qualities and essential Christian attitudes in keeping with scriptural emphasis.
3. Directed in the development of a distinctly Christian lifestyle in obedience to the will of God and the pattern of Christ, and encouraged to live it in the power of the Holy Spirit." (journeyinline.org, 2021)

This call is great, and as we will discuss, serves as a stabilizer for the entire body. Teachers are the holders of sound doctrine. They use this doctrine to impart knowledge to those that they touch. The rise of technology and the global exchange of information has increased the call for sound doctrine. In a time that information can make it to anywhere in the world within seconds, it is easy for error to creep into the body of Christ. Thank God that he never changes and his word remains sure. Teachers are not," swept away by the currents of cultural change" (Trimm, 2018) Let's review this further in the future chapters.

2

What The Book Is Not

This book is not an instruction manual. It is also not meant to be construed as a call. God is the one who calls. If you are called, God will tell you first. I strongly suggest you review your calling with leadership if you are in a church ministry. If you are not, I urge you to review the resource section to get the training and/or support to assist you with walking in your calling. I do not subscribe to the opinion that all teachers need to go to a school of theology. I do believe that a system of mentorship and training is pivotal to the life of the teacher.

This book is also not a curriculum for the call to teach. This is an exploration and research book to explore the calling biblically with some slight discussion of the gift in modern times.

If you are called to teach the Word of God, my prayer is that you will make it your life's priority to manifest. The entire body of Christ is counting on you.

Matthew 9:35-38

   And Jesus went about all the cities and villages, teaching in their synagogues, and preaching the gospel of the kingdom, and healing every sickness and every disease among the people.

But when he saw the multitudes, he was moved with compassion on them, because they fainted, and were scattered abroad, as sheep having no shepherd.

Then saith he unto his disciples, The harvest truly is plenteous, but the labourers are few; Pray ye , therefore, the Lord of the harvest, that he will send forth labourers into his harvest.

Simply put, the reason you have such a genuine love for the Word of God, the reason you filter all prophetic words through the Word of God, the reason you can spot a wrong dividing of the Word of God a mile away is that you are called to teach. The Kingdom of Darkness sees you as if you are walking in your calling, even if you are not. This is why some people seem to have high-level warfare without operating in a high-level calling. Therefore you would be best served to manifest and position yourself properly.

Whether you are a teacher who teaches in a church or other format. Whether you are a teacher who writes books creates courses and videos, or designs biblical tools for the Body of Christ, I pray that this book will fuel a pang of hunger in your soul to manifest. May I pray for you?

May you receive the support and assistance that you need to undergird you in this important calling.

May you bring words of healing and deliverance directly from the throne room of God.

May your character remain strong and stable without controversy.

May your Word level continually increase, and may God grace you with the ability to relay wisdom, knowledge, and understanding with skill and the anointing of the Holy Spirit.

May your light extend into the entirety of the location ordained for you, so that you will be a lighthouse for those drowning in darkness.

In Jesus' name, I pray. Amen.

3

Are You A Teacher?

The book, Marks of a Spiritual Leader, gave a very engaging list of traits that a Bible teacher should have:

1. A good teacher asks himself the hardest questions, works through to answers, and then frames provocative questions for his learners to stimulate their thinking.
2. A good teacher analyzes his subject matter into parts and sees relationships and discovers the unity of the whole.
3. A good teacher knows the problems learners will have with his subject matter and encourages them and gets them over the humps of discouragement.
4. A good teacher foresees objections and thinks them through so that he can answer them intelligently.
5. A good teacher can put himself in the place of a variety of learners and therefore explain hard things in terms that are clear from their standpoint.
6. A good teacher is a concrete, not abstract; specific, not general; precise, not vague; vulnerable, not evasive.
7. A good teacher always asks, "So what?" and tries to see how discoveries shape our whole system of thought. He tries to relate discoveries to life and tries to avoid compartmentalizing.
8. The goal of a good teacher is the transformation of all of life and thought into a Christ-honoring unity." (Piper, 2014)

I would like to add that teachers will love the Word of God. They are the person who emerges from the super-tornado clinging to their books. They will appreciate good teaching. The Bible teacher must be teachable above all.

A good Bible teacher must be willing to pray for a fresh and relevant word for the people. Even if they are given a topic, the effective teacher will still need to seek the Holy Spirit for guidance in crafting effective communication.

4

Teacher vs Preacher

We know that effective preachers weave teaching skillfully in their sermons. The most common question is exactly what is the difference between a preacher and a teacher. Are all teachers preachers and vice-versa? Many of the great generals believe that all preachers must teach as a function of their teaching.

The easy way to differentiate is my small description

Preaching seeks to create the pow
  Teaching seeks to create the wow

Preaching may not always teach you things you don't know. Most sermons should stir up your pure mind by way of remembrance.

2 Peter 3:1-2
  This second epistle, beloved, I now write unto you; in *both* which I stir up your pure minds by way of remembrance: That ye may be mindful of the words which were spoken before by the holy prophets, and of the commandment of us the apostles of the Lord and Saviour:

RC Sproul gave a great analysis of teaching versus preaching.

"Typically, we distinguish between preaching and teaching. Preaching involves such things as exhortation, exposition, admonition, encouragement, and comfort, while teaching is the transfer of information and instruction in various areas of content. In practice, however, there is much overlap between the two. Preaching must communicate content and include teaching, and teaching people the things of God cannot be done in a neutral manner but must exhort them to heed and obey the Word of Christ. God's people need both preaching and teaching" (sermoncentral.com, 2021)

Preaching seeks to connect with your soul. The messages may be meant to excite and drive to action. One example would be a message that advocates its listeners against fornication. The vast majority of saved people know that fornication is wrong. The sermon brings about godly repentance and a softened heart to the commandments of God.

Teaching, on the other hand, should instruct with new information or a new way of looking at known information. A teacher might explain the horrible covenants and legal rights obtained by the Kingdom of Darkness when a person commits fornication. It is not abnormal to see tears with tissues in the hands of the congregation of the preacher. Conversely, it is not abnormal to see pens, paper, and scribbled notes in the hands of the congregation of the teacher.

Biblical Examples of Preaching
  John The Baptist (Matthew 23:33-
  39)
  Paul (1 Corinthians 15)
  Stephen (Acts 6:8-10)
  Jesus (Matthew 23:13-29)

Biblical Examples of Teaching
  Jesus (Matthew 6:5)
  Paul (Galatians 3:1)

Prophetic Insights on Teaching
In addition, teachers often operate with Words of Wisdom and Words of knowledge, even though they are not prophets. The difference is in the administration of the gift. Teachers and teaching preachers will often receive a scripture for a word for the entire congregation and it will be relayed corporately during their message. This may not seem like the traditional way of conveying these utterances, but understand that effective teachers must be strongly influenced by the Spirit of Wisdom, The Spirit of Knowledge, and

the Spirit of Understanding. The reason for this is that these spirits must be present in the environment to prepare the hearts of the gathering to receive the Word of God.

💡 Try it out: When you read the previous paragraph, it may have contained information that you have never heard before. Pray to loose the Spirits of Knowledge, Understanding, and Wisdom. Read it again. If you are motivated, loose these spirits plus the Spirit of Counsel into the person or people who preach and teach the Word of God to you.

⚡The spiritual teacher needs power. Three types of spirits combat the evil Spirits of Fears, these are Spirits of Power, Love, and Sound Mind. The Spirits of Wisdom, Knowledge, Understanding, Counsel, Might, and Fear of the Lord are all Spirits of Power. When you are flanked with these militant spirits you operate in a power that can disarm the power of the enemy. Did you know that teaching was so violent?

5

Types of Teachers

The teaching gift may easily be the most versatile of all of the five-fold mandates. Common uses include:

Teachers who Pastor

Sunday School Teachers

Writers

Course Developers

Secular Teachers

Professors

Apostolic Teacher- These teachers work in the establishment and building of educational systems. We saw this during the reformation when major universities were established by churches. One example would be Pat Robertson who founded Regents University as well as CBN and the much-watched 700 Club.

Prophetic Teacher- These teachers generally receive scriptures prophetically. The teaching is fresh and full of deliverance. Jesus operated in this teaching dimension.

Evangelistic Teachers- These teachers travel and instruct the body. They may be led to areas of spiritual errors with the light of the Word of God.

Pastoral Teachers will shepherd and oversee ministries with the light of the Word of God.

Whatever way a teacher manifests, they work to shine the light of God's word.

6

Five-fold Quick Guide

Five-fold Ministry

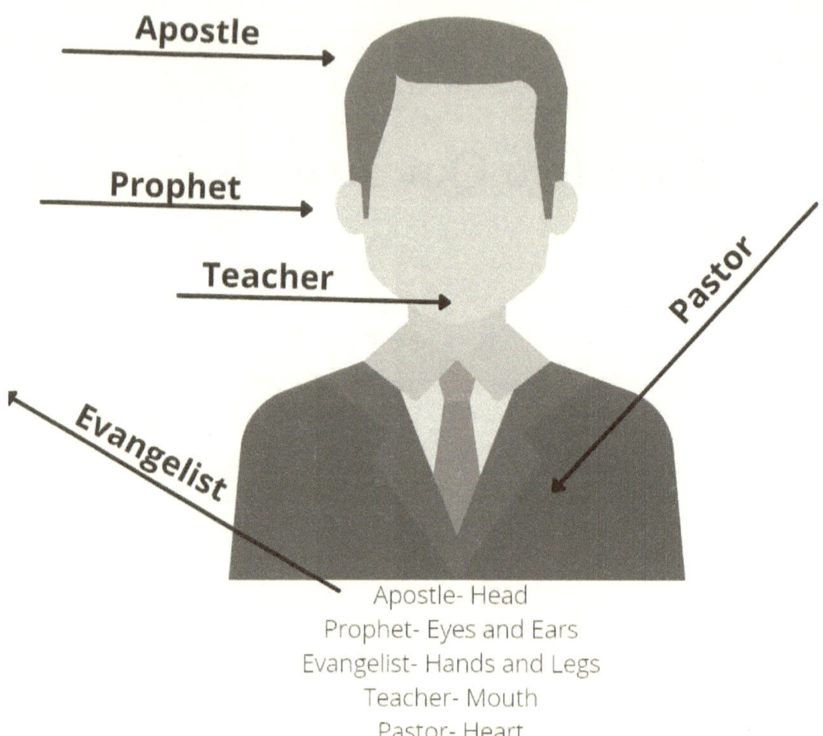

The offices of the five-fold ministry are not titles. There is an erroneous belief that a person is promoted from one level in the five-fold ministry and to another. You will often hear me speak of the apostolic ministry as a high calling. I simply mean that there is a lot of high-level warfare and responsibility. That notwithstanding you are not promoted from prophet to apostle. They are two completely different offices.

A good analogy would be:
 Apostle- Doctor
 Prophet- Lawyer

Evangelist- Politician
Teacher- Nuclear Physicist
Pastor- Engineer

Each position has its merit. Unlike positional offices such as bishop and deacon, which can be obtained by an election and are subject to promotion. The work defines the office.

<u>Basic Job Description</u>

Apostle- Build Establish Cover

Prophet- See Hear Relay

Evangelist- Awaken Influence Shift

Teacher- Exhort Interpret Translate

Pastor- Lead Parent Align and Plant

<u>Ephesians 5:11-13</u>

And he gave some, apostles; and some, prophets; and some, evangelists; and some, pastors and teachers;

12 For the perfecting of the saints, for the work of the ministry, for the edifying of the body of Christ:

13 Till we all come in the unity of the faith, and of the knowledge of the Son of God, unto a perfect man, unto the measure of the stature of the fulness of Christ:

Teachers do not simply develop new converts. They also develop other teachers and the Body of Christ. A convert that enters into the body is sent through an invisible assembly line of development. Teachers are pivotal to this process. Teachers also assist in filtering prophetic words through the Word of God as a defense against error and evil winds of doctrine.

1 Corinthians 3:5-9

5What then is Apollos? And what is Paul? They are servants through whom you believed, as the Lord has assigned to each his role. 6I planted the seed and Apollos watered it, but God made it grow. 7So neither he who plants nor he who waters is anything, but only God, who makes things grow. 8He who plants and he who waters are one in purpose, a and each will be rewarded according to his labor. 9For we are God's fellow workers; you are God's field, God's building.

7

The Stabilizing Teacher

The office of the teacher can be likened to the tent pegs. Teachers will intentionally and unintentionally filter all words through the lens of the Word of God. Bible teachers are a necessary part of every assembly. They are the testers of doctrine for soundness. Where the voice of the teacher is silenced, strange and errant doctrine stands the chance of creeping into the church by sidestepping the lens of the Word of God.

If we compare the five-fold ministry to a house, the teaching mandate would be the foundation. The prophetical aspects of other folds have a real danger of entering into error without the stabilizing force of the Word of God.

This is important, due to the fact that Jesus made it clear that the knowledge of his voice is paramount to people who consider themselves his sheep.

John 10:27

26But ye believe not, because ye are not of my sheep, as I said unto you. 27My sheep hear my voice, and I know them, and they follow me: 28And I give unto them eternal life, and they shall never perish, neither shall any man pluck them out of my hand. 29My Father, which gave them me, is greater than all; and no man is able to pluck them out of my Father's hand. 30I and my Father are one.

This scripture used to worry me. What if I missed his voice? I knew that evil powers can potentially mimic the voice of God, and even had the potential to mimic my voice. What if I missed it? Praise God that Jesus did not leave this up to chance. He never intended for us to rely on our physical sense of hearing to know his voice. Let me explain...

Jesus is only one temporal name for the Messiah. His eternal name is and always will be the Living Word. This means that from the beginning we had the Word. The voice of the Word is the Word. The sheep of God will not follow a stranger because they know the Word! Hang on teachers, this is where you come in.

Romans 10:14

How then shall they call on him in whom they have not believed? and how shall they believe in him of whom they have not heard? and how shall they hear without a preacher?

This means that every time you teach the Word of God you are introducing the people to Jesus. They won't follow a stranger because you have introduced them to the true voice of God. This is the same theory whether it is a Sunday school of preschool children or a seniors bible study. The teachers have the heavy responsibility to ensure Jesus is properly introduced to the body. Much like someone who has recorded conversations with a person and can therefore decipher when a voice does not match the original, the teacher carries the voice of God and has the express gift of discerning all prophecies based upon that voice for accuracy. This may put the teaching mandate at odds with other mandates. The manifested teacher accepts this as par for the course.

No matter the location of the doctrine, a review of cults will expose a lack of true Bible teachers or Bible teachers who are so disempowered, that the Word of God has no real unfiltered outlet to send fresh Rhema, and halt the flow of bad information and faulty doctrine that undergirds so many cults and quite a few cult-like churches

This in action:

Background: Paul was sending an exhortation to Galatians who practiced circumcision with the motive of adhering to the Law.

Galatians 5:1-15

"Hold fast therefore in the liberty wherewith Christ hath made us free, and be not entangled again with the yoke of bondage.

Behold, I Paul say unto you, that if ye be circumcised, Christ shall profit you nothing. For I testify again to every man that is circumcised, that he is a debtor to do the whole law. Christ has become of no effect unto you, whosoever of you are justified by the law; ye are fallen from grace. For we through the Spirit wait for the hope of righteousness by faith. For in Jesus Christ neither circumcision availeth any thing, nor uncircumcision; but faith which worketh by love.

Ye did run well; who did hinder you that ye should not obey the truth? This persuasion cometh not of him that calleth you. A little leaven leaveneth the whole lump. I have confidence in you through the Lord, that ye will be none otherwise minded: but he that troubleth you shall bear his judgment, whosoever he be. And I, brethren, if I yet preach circumcision, why do I yet suffer persecution? then is the offence of the cross ceased. I would they were even cut off which trouble you.

For, brethren, ye have been called unto liberty; only use not liberty for an occasion to the flesh, but by love serve one another. For all the law is fulfilled in one word, even in this; Thou shalt love thy neighbour as thyself. But if ye bite and devour one another, take heed that ye be not consumed one of another."

Modern Day Example

The Olde Day non-denominational church believes that the Bible allows polygamy. The men in the ministry have no less than five wives each. Teaching that this is against the Word of God will cause all sorts of trouble for the teacher and could result in the teacher being excommunicated. The church in this case has shut out the voice of Jesus. The minds of the people are not being renewed. The reason is that the teaching gift is being blocked from its checks and balances effect. This effect is erroneous and rigid theology.

It is easy to argue that the teaching calling may be one of the most important in the Body of Christ. Teachers are the handlers of the voice of Jesus. The successful teacher is a bridge to transmit the voice of Jesus, versus being a gate. In the case of Olde Day church, the structure of the church has been established to shut out any dissenting voice, even the voice of Jesus.

8

Wisdom Knowledge and Understanding

I expected a variation in the dictionary definitions of wisdom, knowledge, and understanding. This was correct because these concepts operate on several levels in the human experience. They are first and foremost spiritual people with an assignment to bless the people. They are systems in which growth, development, and even our world are formed. (Proverbs 3:19). They are the foundation of the teaching gift. This is the impartation from the Holy Spirit that must rest on the head of all teachers.

<u>Wisdom</u>

Wisdom is so often personified as an ignored woman crying for the audience of stubborn people. She does not offer only her presence, she also offers length of days and riches to those who will heed her counsel. (Proverbs 1:20-33)

Wisdom has several definitions which include:

the quality of having experience, knowledge, and good judgment; the quality of being wise.
   "listen to his words of wisdom"

the soundness of an action or decision with regard to the application of experience, knowledge, and good judgment.

the body of knowledge and principles that develops within a specified society or period.

    a. ability to discern inner qualities and relationships: INSIGHT
  b: good sense: JUDGMENT
  c: generally accepted belief
  d: accumulated philosophical or scientific learning: KNOWLEDGE
  2: a wise attitude, belief, or course of action
  3: the teachings of the ancient wise men

the ability to use your knowledge and experience to make good decisions and judgments:

sagacity
sageness
intelligence
understanding
insight
perception
perceptiveness
percipience
perspicuity
acuity
discernment
sense
common sense
shrewdness
astuteness
acumen
smartness
judiciousness
judgment
foresight
clear-sightedness
prudence
circumspection
logic
rationale
rationality
soundness
saneness
advisability

sharpness

savvy

smarts

A bit about wisdom

Sophia-The word originates from the word σοφός. Sophia- is not simply the Wisdom of godly things. It is wisdom in all spheres.

σοφία sophía, sof-ee'-ah; from G4680; wisdom (higher or lower, worldly or spiritual):—wisdom.

More than all of the other giftings, the teacher must operate in Wisdom. After all, God gives the lesson but grace and delivery are often in the hands of the teacher.

Knowledge

The Greek word for knowledge is *gnōsis* (a feminine noun derived from 1097 /*ginōskō*, "experientially know") – *functional* ("working") knowledge gleaned from first-hand (personal) experience, connecting theory to the application; "application-knowledge," gained in (by) a direct relationship.

The definition of knowledge is facts, information, and skills acquired by a person through experience or education; the theoretical or practical understanding of a subject.

To streamline this definition would be to define a teacher as someone who has taken the time to inform themselves in and about God, and has experienced the presence of God. This person then takes these interactions and uses them to build others.

Understanding

The Greek word for understanding is φρόνησις

Biblical understanding is that (which leads to right action), practical wisdom, prudence.

The definition of knowledge is

 : the fact or condition of knowing something with familiarity gained through experience or association

(2): acquaintance with or understanding of science, art, or technique

b(1): the fact or condition of being aware of something

(2): the range of one's information or understanding answered to the best of my *knowledge*: the circumstance or condition of apprehending truth or fact through reasoning :

d: the fact or condition of having information or of being learned. a person of unusual knowledge.

<u>The Big Picture</u>

Why does a teacher read and study more than the average layperson? It is because they are worksmen. (2 Timothy 2:15) The knowledge imparted by the teacher will help develop, keep, and empower the lives of the hearers.

Dr. Myles Munroe spoke of having 987 invitations for a year that had not even begun. What makes the world reach past so many available options to hear from one source? I feel it is Wisdom, Knowledge, and Understanding. The world is hungry for these dimensions of grace. This desire puts manifested Bible teachers in high demand.

Proverbs 4:7

Wisdom is the principal thing; therefore get wisdom: and with all thy getting get understanding.

The Bible teacher holds the keys to transform lives. Their life experience and spiritual intercourse with God serve as a bridge to bring others into a higher communion with God. In addition, teachers train leaders. No person should rise into leadership without a teacher. King Saul is an example of entering leadership without training. He lost his kingdom for breaking protocol. Further, the character development to gracefully yield to the command of God was not resident in Saul. He was the first king. There was not another king for Saul to observe and learn. It was necessary that he heed Samuel's instructions, which were being relayed directly from God. Unfortunately for Saul, he did not. The result was the loss of the kingdom.

Jesus took the time to teach the kingdom by Word and demonstration. He relayed the Word and the experience. This experience shifted the mindset of the apostles and transformed their character. The amazing thing about learning through teaching is that some knowledge enters the hearers unknown. This information may go on to be transferred generationally. For their part, the teacher may be unaware of the impact that their lesson made in the lives of the future generations of the people who learn from them.

9

Resources

Training

https://trainbibleteachers.com/teachers.htm

https://iblp.org/questions/what-are-common-characteristics-teachers

https://gewatkins.net/qualities-of-a-bible-class-teacher/

https://mintools.com/preview-tt4.htm

https://bibletalk.tv/

Moody Bible Institute

https://www.calvinseminary.edu/academics/certificate-in-bible-instruction

For Youngsters
https://www.rce-international.org/

https://www.aacs.org/

https://www.actsschools.org/

II

Scriptural Quick Reference

10

Biblical Words for Teachers

Titus 2:7-8 ESV

Show yourself in all respects to be a model of good works, and in your teaching show integrity, dignity, and sound speech that cannot be condemned, so that an opponent may be put to shame, having nothing evil to say about us.

Proverbs 22:6 ESV

Train up a child in the way he should go; even when he is old he will not depart from it.

James 3:1-2 ESV

Not many of you should become teachers, my brothers, for you know that we who teach will be judged with greater strictness. For we all stumble in many ways. And if anyone does not stumble in what he says, he is a perfect man, able also to bridle his whole body.

Luke 6:40 ESV

A disciple is not above his teacher, but everyone when he is fully trained will be like his teacher.

1 Peter 4:10 ESV

As each has received a gift, use it to serve one another, as good stewards of God's varied grace:

Psalm 32:8

I will instruct you and teach you in the way you should go; I will counsel you with my eye upon you.

Deuteronomy 32:2

May my teaching drop as the rain, my speech distill as the dew, like gentle rain upon the tender grass, and like showers upon the herb.

2 Timothy 2:15 ESV

Do your best to present yourself to God as one approved, a worker who has no need to be ashamed, rightly handling the word of truth.

2 Timothy 3:16 ESV

All Scripture is breathed out by God and profitable for teaching, for reproof, for correction, and for training in righteousness,

Romans 12:6-7 ESV

Having gifts that differ according to the grace given to us, let us use them: if prophecy, in proportion to our faith; if service, in our serving; the one who teaches, in his teaching;

Romans 12:7 ESV

If service, in our serving; the one who teaches, in his teaching;

1 Corinthians 15:58 ESV

Therefore, my beloved brothers, be steadfast, immovable, always abounding in the work of the Lord, knowing that in the Lord your labor is not in vain.

Matthew 5:19 ESV

Therefore whoever relaxes one of the least of these commandments and teaches others to do the same will be called least in the kingdom of heaven, but whoever does them and teaches them will be called great in the kingdom of heaven.

Matthew 28:20

Teaching them to observe all that I have commanded you. And behold, I am with you always, to the end of the age."

1 Corinthians 12:28 ESV

And God has appointed in the church first apostles, second prophets, third teachers, then miracles, then gifts of healing, helping, administrating, and various kinds of tongues.

Colossians 3:16 ESV

Let the word of Christ dwell in you richly, teaching and admonishing one another in all wisdom, singing psalms and hymns and spiritual songs, with thankfulness in your hearts to God.

2 Timothy 2:2 ESV

And what you have heard from me in the presence of many witnesses entrust to faithful men who will be able to teach others also.

Ephesians 4:11-16

And he gave the apostles, the prophets, the evangelists, the shepherds and teachers, to equip the saints for the work of ministry, for building up the body of Christ, until we all attain to the unity of the faith and of the knowledge of the Son of God, to mature manhood, to the measure of the stature of the fullness of Christ, so that we may no longer be children, tossed to and fro by the waves and carried about by every wind of doctrine, by human cunning, by craftiness in deceitful schemes. Rather, speaking the truth in love, we are to grow up in every way into him who is the head, into Christ, ...

James 3:1 ESV

Not many of you should become teachers, my brothers, for you know that we who teach will be judged with greater strictness.

Romans 2:21 ESV

You then who teach others, do you not teach yourself? While you preach against stealing, do you steal?

1 Timothy 4:11 ESV

Command and teach these things.

Psalm 119:99 ESV

I have more understanding than all my teachers, for your testimonies are my meditation.

2 Timothy 3:16-17 ESV

All Scripture is breathed out by God and profitable for teaching, for reproof, for correction, and for training in righteousness, that the man of God may be competent, equipped for every good work.

2 Timothy 1:11

For which I was appointed a preacher and apostle and teacher,

Galatians 6:6 ESV

One who is taught the word must share all good things with the one who teaches.

1 Timothy 1:7 ESV

Desiring to be teachers of the law, without understanding either what they are saying or the things about which they make confident assertions.

Ephesians 4:11 ESV

And he gave the apostles, the prophets, the evangelists, the shepherds and teachers,

2 Timothy 4:2 ESV

Preach the word; be ready in season and out of season; reprove, rebuke, and exhort, with complete patience and teaching.

Ephesians 3:16-19 ESV

That according to the riches of his glory he may grant you to be strengthened with power through his Spirit in your inner being, so that Christ may dwell in your hearts through faith—that you, being rooted and grounded in love, may have strength to comprehend with all the saints what is the breadth and length and height and depth, and to know the love of Christ that surpasses knowledge, that you may be filled with all the fullness of God.

Proverbs 11:25 ESV / 64 helpful votes

Whoever brings blessing will be enriched, and one who waters will himself be watered.

Luke 12:12 ESV / 60 helpful votes

For the Holy Spirit will teach you in that very hour what you ought to say."

1 Corinthians 14:26 ESV

What then, brothers? When you come together, each one has a hymn, a lesson, a revelation, a tongue, or an interpretation. Let all things be done for building up.

1 Timothy 1:7-8 ESV

Desiring to be teachers of the law, without understanding either what they are saying or the things about which they make confident assertions. Now we know that the law is good, if one uses it lawfully,

Colossians 1:28 ESV

Him we proclaim, warning everyone and teaching everyone with all wisdom, that we may present everyone mature in Christ.

1 Peter 3:15 ESV

But in your hearts honor Christ the Lord as holy, always being prepared to make a defense to anyone who asks you for a reason for the hope that is in you; yet do it with gentleness and respect,

1 Corinthians 12:29 ESV

Are all apostles? Are all prophets? Are all teachers? Do all work miracles?

1 Corinthians 9:27 ESV

But I discipline my body and keep it under control, lest after preaching to others I myself should be disqualified.

3 John 1:3 ESV / 48

For I rejoiced greatly when the brothers came and testified to your truth, as indeed you are walking in the truth.

1 Thessalonians 1:2 ESV

We give thanks to God always for all of you, constantly mentioning you in our prayers,

1 Chronicles 16:11 ESV

Seek the Lord and his strength; seek his presence continually!

Jeremiah 17:8 ESV

He is like a tree planted by water, that sends out its roots by the stream, and does not fear when heat comes, for its leaves remain green, and is not anxious in the year of drought, for it does not cease to bear fruit."

Romans 2:20 ESV

An instructor of the foolish, a teacher of children, having in the law the embodiment of knowledge and truth—

Psalm 37:31 ESV

The law of his God is in his heart; his steps do not slip.

Deuteronomy 6:7 ESV

You shall teach them diligently to your children, and shall talk of them when you sit in your house, and when you walk by the way, and when you lie down, and when you rise.

Titus 2:7 ESV

Show yourself in all respects to be a model of good works, and in your teaching show integrity, dignity,

Philippians 3:12-14 ESV

Not that I have already obtained this or am already perfect, but I press on to make it my own, because Christ Jesus has made me his own. Brothers, I do not consider that I have made it my own. But one thing I do: forgetting what lies behind and straining forward to what lies ahead, I press on toward the goal for the prize of the upward call of God in Christ Jesus.

Exodus 4:12 ESV

Now therefore go, and I will be with your mouth and teach you what you shall speak."

2 Timothy 3:14-17 ESV

But as for you, continue in what you have learned and have firmly believed, knowing from whom you learned it and how from childhood you have been acquainted with the sacred writings, which are able to make you wise for salvation through faith in Christ Jesus. All Scripture is breathed out by God and profitable for teaching, for reproof, for correction, and for training in righteousness, that the man of God may be competent, equipped for every good work.

Nehemiah 8:8 ESV

They read from the book, from the Law of God, clearly, and they gave the sense, so that the people understood the reading.

Deuteronomy 11:18-19 ESV

"You shall therefore lay up these words of mine in your heart and in your soul, and you shall bind them as a sign on your hand, and they shall be as frontlets between your eyes. You shall teach them to your children, talking of them when you are sitting in your house, and when you are walking by the way, and when you lie down, and when you rise.

1 Samuel 12:23 ESV

Moreover, as for me, far be it from me that I should sin against the Lord by ceasing to pray for you, and I will instruct you in the good and the right way.

11

Knowledge Scriptures

Proverbs 2:6

For the Lord giveth wisdom: out of his mouth cometh knowledge and understanding.

Proverbs 12:1-

Whoso loveth instruction loveth knowledge: but he that hateth reproof is brutish.

Ecclesiastes 1:18-

For in much wisdom is much grief: and he that increaseth knowledge increaseth sorrow.

Proverbs 1:7-

The fear of the Lord is the beginning of knowledge: but fools despise wisdom and instruction.

Proverbs 9:10-

The fear of the Lord is the beginning of wisdom: and the knowledge of the holy is understanding.

Proverbs 11:9-

An hypocrite with his mouth destroyeth his neighbour: but through knowledge shall the just be delivered.

2 Peter 1:5-7-

And beside this, giving all diligence, add to your faith virtue; and to virtue knowledge;

And to knowledge temperance; and to temperance patience; and to patience godliness; And to godliness brotherly kindness; and to brotherly kindness charity.

2 Peter 3:18-

But grow in grace, and in the knowledge of our Lord and Saviour Jesus Christ. To him be glory both now and for ever. Amen.

Romans 11:33-

O the depth of the riches both of the wisdom and knowledge of God! how unsearchable are his judgments, and his ways past finding out!

1 Corinthians 15:34-

Awake to righteousness, and sin not; for some have not the knowledge of God: I speak this to your shame.

Romans 3:20-

Therefore by the deeds of the law there shall no flesh be justified in his sight: for by the law is the knowledge of sin.

Psalm 19:1-2-

The heavens declare the glory of God; and the firmament sheweth his handywork. Day unto day uttereth speech, and night unto night sheweth knowledge.

2 Peter 1:3-

According as his divine power hath given unto us all things that pertain unto life and godliness, through the knowledge of him that hath called us to glory and virtue.

Ephesians 1:17-

That the God of our Lord Jesus Christ, the Father of glory, may give unto you the spirit of wisdom and revelation in the knowledge of him.

1 Corinthians 13:2-

And though I have the gift of prophecy, and understand all mysteries, and all knowledge; and though I have all faith, so that I could remove mountains, and have not charity, I am nothing.

Colossians 3:9-10-

Lie not one to another, seeing that ye have put off the old man with his deeds; And have put on the new man, which is renewed in knowledge after the image of him that created him.

1 Peter 3:7-

So shall the knowledge of wisdom be unto thy soul: when thou hast found it, then there shall be a reward, and thy expectation shall not be cut off.

Colossians 2:2-

That their hearts might be comforted, being knit together in love, and unto all riches of the full assurance of understanding, to the acknowledgement of the mystery of God, and of the Father, and of Christ.

(Dailyverses.net, 2021)

Proverbs 18:15 -

The heart of the prudent getteth knowledge; and the ear of the wise seeketh knowledge.

Proverbs 1:7 -

The fear of the LORD is the beginning of knowledge: but fools despise wisdom and instruction.

Proverbs 2:10 -

When wisdom entereth into thine heart, and knowledge is pleasant unto thy soul;

Hosea 4:6-7 -

My people are destroyed for lack of knowledge: because thou hast rejected knowledge, I will also reject thee, that thou shalt be no priest to me: seeing thou hast forgotten the law of thy God, I will also forget thy children. (Read More...)

Proverbs 24:5 -

A wise man is strong; yea, a man of knowledge increaseth strength.

Proverbs 8:10 -

Receive my instruction, and not silver; and knowledge rather than choice gold.

Proverbs 15:14 -

The heart of him that hath understanding seeketh knowledge: but the mouth of fools feedeth on foolishness.

Proverbs 3:1-35 -

My son, forget not my law; but let thine heart keep my commandments: (Read More...)

Proverbs 12:1 -

Whoso loveth instruction loveth knowledge: but he that hateth reproof is brutish.

Proverbs 2:1-22 -

My son, if thou wilt receive my words, and hide my commandments with thee; (Read More...)

Hosea 4:6 -

My people are destroyed for lack of knowledge: because thou hast rejected knowledge, I will also reject thee, that thou shalt be no priest to me: seeing thou hast forgotten the law of thy God, I will also forget thy children.

Psalms 119:66 -

Teach me good judgment and knowledge: for I have believed thy commandments.

1 Corinthians 12:8 -

For to one is given by the Spirit the word of wisdom; to another the word of knowledge by the same Spirit

(kingjamesbibleonline.com,2021)

12

Wisdom Scriptures

Solomon had the insight to ask for wisdom to lead God's people. The wisest man is the man who takes the time to receive the wisdom of the Lord. I urge every child of God that seeks to manifest to at least read these scriptures.

2 Chronicles 1:10

Give me now wisdom and knowledge, that I may go out and come in before this people: for who can judge this thy people, that is so great?

Wisdom/Chokmah/Chakam

Why Wisdom?

Proverbs 1:2

To know wisdom and instruction; to perceive the words of understanding;

Proverbs 1:3

To receive the instruction of wisdom, justice, and judgment, and equity;

How to be Wise

Proverbs 18:1

Through desire a man, having separated himself, seeketh and intermeddleth with all wisdom

Proverbs 1:7

The fear of the Lord is the beginning of knowledge: but fools despise wisdom and instruction.

Job 28:28

And unto man he said, Behold, the fear of the Lord, that is wisdom; and to depart from evil is understanding.

Psalm 111:10

The fear of the Lord is the beginning of wisdom: a good understanding has all that do his commandments: his praise endureth forever.

Proverbs 8:12

In wisdom dwell with prudence and find out knowledge of witty inventions.

Proverbs 8:14

Counsel is mine, and sound wisdom: I am understanding; I have strength.

Proverbs 9:10

The fear of the Lord is the beginning of wisdom: and the knowledge of the holy is understanding.

Proverbs 1:2

To know wisdom and instruction; to perceive the words of understanding;

Proverbs 1:3

To receive the instruction of wisdom, justice, and judgment, and equity;

Proverbs 1:7

The fear of the Lord is the beginning of knowledge: but fools despise wisdom and instruction.

Proverbs 1:20

Wisdom crieth without; she uttereth her voice in the streets:

Proverbs 2:2

So that thou incline thine ear unto wisdom, and apply thine heart to understanding;

Proverbs 2:6

For the Lord giveth wisdom: out of his mouth cometh knowledge and understanding.

Proverbs 2:7

He lays sound wisdom for the righteous: he is a buckler to them that walk uprightly.

Proverbs 2:10

When wisdom entereth into thine heart, and knowledge is pleasant unto thy soul;

Proverbs 3:13

Happy is the man that findeth wisdom, and the man that getteth understanding.

Proverbs 3:19

The Lord by wisdom hath founded the earth; by understanding hath he established the heavens.

Proverbs 3:21

My son, let not them depart from thine eyes: keep sound wisdom and discretion:

Proverbs 4:5

Get wisdom, get understanding: forget it not; neither decline from the words of my mouth.

Proverbs 4:7

Wisdom is the principal thing; therefore get wisdom: and with all thy getting get understanding.

Proverbs 4:11

I have taught thee in the way of wisdom; I have led thee in the right paths.

Proverbs 7:4

Say unto wisdom, Thou art my sister; and call understanding thy kinswoman:

Proverbs 8:1

Doth not wisdom cry? and understanding put forth her voice?

Proverbs 8:5

O ye simple, understand wisdom: and, ye fools, be ye of an understanding heart.

Proverbs 8:11

For wisdom is better than rubies; and all the things that may be desired are not to be compared to it.

The Character of Godly Wisdom

James 3:17

But the wisdom that is from above is first pure, then peaceable, gentle, and easy to be intreated, full of mercy and good fruits, without partiality, and without hypocrisy.

Proverbs 9:1

Wisdom hath builded her house, she hath hewn out her seven pillars:

Proverbs 15:21

Folly is joy to him that is destitute of wisdom: but a man of understanding walketh uprightly.

Proverbs 15:33

The fear of the Lord is the instruction of wisdom; and before honour is humility.

Proverbs 16:16

How much better is it to get wisdom than gold! and to get understanding rather than to be chosen than silver!

Proverbs 17:16

Wherefore is there a price in the hand of a fool to get wisdom, seeing he hath no heart to it?

Proverbs 17:24

Wisdom is before him that hath understanding; but the eyes of a fool are in the ends of the earth.

Romans 11:33

O the depth of the riches both of In Context and knowledge of God! how unsearchable are his judgments, and his ways past finding out!

Jeremiah 51:15

He hath made the earth by his power, he hath established the world by his wisdom, and hath stretched out the heaven by his understanding.

Job 32:7

I said, Days should speak, and multitude of years should teach wisdom

Job 36:5

Behold, God is mighty, and despiseth not any: he is mighty in strength and wisdom.

Job 38:36

Who hath put wisdom in the inward parts? or who hath given understanding to the heart?

Jeremiah 10:12

He hath made the earth by his power, he hath established the world by his wisdom, and hath stretched out the heavens by his discretion.

Job 11:6

And that he would shew thee the secrets of wisdom, that they are double to that which is! Know therefore that God exacteth of thee less than thine iniquity deserveth.

Job 12:12

With the ancient is wisdom; and in length of days understanding.

Job 12:13

With him is wisdom and strength, he hath counsel and understanding.

Job 12:16

With him is strength and wisdom: the deceived and the deceiver are his.

Isaiah 29:14

Therefore, behold, I will proceed to do a marvellous work among these people, even a marvellous work and a wonder: for the wisdom of their wise men shall perish, and the understanding of their prudent men shall be hid.

Isaiah 33:6

And wisdom and knowledge shall be the stability of thy times, and strength of salvation: the fear of the Lord is his treasure.

1 Corinthians 1:24

But unto them which are called, both Jews and Greeks, Christ the power of God, and the wisdom of God.

Luke 7:35

But wisdom is justified by all her children.

Luke 11:31

The queen of the south shall rise up in judgment?? with the men of this generation, and condemn them: for she came from the utmost parts of the earth to hear the wisdom of Solomon; and, behold, a greater than Solomon is here.

Ecclesiastes 10:10

If the iron be blunt, and he do not whet the edge, then must he put to more strength: but wisdom is profitable to direct.

Proverbs 10:13

In the lips of him that hath understanding wisdom is found: but a rod is for the back of him that is void of understanding.

Proverbs 10:21

The lips of the righteous feed many: but fools die for want of wisdom.

Proverbs 10:23

It is as sport to a fool to do mischief: but a man of understanding hath wisdom.

Proverbs 10:31

The mouth of the just bringeth forth wisdom: but the froward tongue shall be cut out.

Proverbs 11:2

When pride cometh, then cometh shame: but with the lowly is wisdom.

Proverbs 11:12

He that is void of wisdom despiseth his neighbour: but a man of understanding holdeth his peace.

Proverbs 12:8

A man shall be commended according to his wisdom: but he that is of a perverse heart shall be despised.

Proverbs 13:10

Only by pride cometh contention: but with the well advised is wisdom.

Proverbs 14:6

A scorner seeketh wisdom, and findeth it not: but knowledge is easy unto him that understandeth.

Proverbs 14:8

The wisdom of the prudent is to understand his way: but the folly of fools is deceit.

Proverbs 14:33

Wisdom resteth in the heart of him that hath understanding: but that which is in the midst of fools is made known.

Isaiah 10:13

For he saith, By the strength of my hand I have done it, and by my wisdom; for I am prudent: and I have removed the bounds of the people, and have robbed their treasures, and I have put down the inhabitants like a valiant man:

Isaiah 11:2

And the spirit of the Lord shall rest upon him, the spirit of wisdom and understanding, the spirit of counsel and might, the spirit of knowledge and of the fear of the Lord;

The Character of Worldly Wisdom

James 3:15

This wisdom descendeth not from above, but is earthly, sensual, devilish.

Job 4:21

Doth not their excellency which is in them go away? they die, even without wisdom.

Job 32:13

Lest ye should say, We have found out wisdom: God thrusteth him down, not man.

Ecclesiastes 2:21

For there is a man whose labour is in wisdom, and in knowledge, and in equity; yet to a man that hath not laboured therein shall he leave it for his portion. This also is vanity and a great evil.

Ecclesiastes 2:26

For God giveth to a man that is good in his sight wisdom, and knowledge, and joy: but to the sinner he giveth travail, to gather and to heap up, that he may give to him that is good before God. This also is vanity and vexation of spirit.

Job 6:13

Is not my help in me? and is wisdom driven quite from me?

Isaiah 47:10

For thou hast trusted in thy wickedness: thou hast said, None seeth me. Thy wisdom and thy knowledge, it hath perverted thee; and thou hast said in thine heart, I am, and none else beside me.

Jeremiah 8:9

The wise men are ashamed, they are dismayed and taken: lo, they have rejected the word of the Lord; and what wisdom is in them?

Jeremiah 9:23

Thus saith the Lord, Let not the wise man glory in his wisdom, neither let the mighty man glory in his might, let not the rich man glory in his riches:

Jeremiah 49:7

Concerning Edom, thus saith the Lord of hosts; Is wisdom no more in Teman? is counsel perished from the prudent? is their wisdom vanished?

1 Corinthians 1:22

For the Jews require a sign, and the Greeks seek after wisdom:

1 Corinthians 1:19

For it is written, I will destroy the wisdom of the wise, and will bring to nothing the understanding of the prudent.

1 Corinthians 1:20

Where is the wise? where is the scribe? where is the disputer of this world? hath not God made foolish the wisdom of this world?

1 Corinthians 1:21

For after that in the wisdom of God the world by wisdom knew not God, it pleased God by the foolishness of preaching to save them that believe.

Acts 7:10

And delivered him out of all his afflictions, and gave him favour and wisdom in the sight of Pharaoh king of Egypt; and he made him governor over Egypt and all his house.

Acts 7:22

And Moses was learned in all the wisdom of the Egyptians, and was mighty in words and in deeds.

(Satan's Wisdom)

Ezekiel 28:12

Son of man, take up a lamentation upon the king of Tyrus, and say unto him, Thus saith the Lord God; Thou sealest up the sum, full of wisdom, and perfect in beauty.

Ezekiel 28:17

Thine heart was lifted up because of thy beauty, thou hast corrupted thy wisdom by reason of thy brightness: I will cast thee to the ground, I will lay thee before kings, that they may behold thee.

Ezekiel 28:4

With thy wisdom and with thine understanding thou hast gotten thee riches, and hast gotten gold and silver into thy treasures:

Ezekiel 28:5

By thy great wisdom and by thy traffick hast thou increased thy riches, and thine heart is lifted up because of thy riches:

Ezekiel 28:7

Behold, therefore I will bring strangers upon thee, the terrible of the nations: and they shall draw their swords against the beauty of thy wisdom, and they shall defile thy brightness.

Acts of Wisdom

Colossians 1:9

For this cause we also, since the day we heard it, do not cease to pray for you, and to desire that ye might be filled with the knowledge of his will in all wisdom and spiritual understanding;

Colossians 1:28

Whom we preach, warning every man, and teaching every man in all wisdom; that we may present every man perfect in Christ Jesus

Colossians 2:3

In whom are hid all the treasures of wisdom and knowledge.

Colossians 2:23

Which things have indeed a shew of wisdom in will worship, and humility, and neglecting of the body: not in any honour to the satisfying of the flesh.

Colossians 3:16

Let the word of Christ dwell in you richly in all wisdom; teaching and admonishing one another in psalms and hymns and spiritual songs, singing with grace in your hearts to the Lord.

Colossians 4:5

Walk in wisdom toward them that are without, redeeming the time.

James 1:5

If any of you lack wisdom, let him ask of God, that giveth to all men liberally, and upbraideth not; and it shall be given him.

James 3:13

Who is a wise man and endued with knowledge among you? let him shew out of a good conversation his works with meekness of wisdom.

2 Corinthians 1:12

For our rejoicing is this, the testimony of our conscience, that in simplicity and godly sincerity, not with fleshly wisdom, but by the grace of God, we have had our conversation in the world, and more abundantly to you-ward.

Ephesians 1:8

Wherein he hath abounded toward us in all wisdom and prudence;

1 Corinthians 2:1

And I, brethren, when I came to you, came not with excellency of speech or of wisdom, declaring unto you the testimony of God.

1 Corinthians 2:4

And my speech and my preaching was not with enticing words of man's wisdom, but in demonstration of the Spirit and of power:

1 Corinthians 2:5
That your faith should not stand in the wisdom of men, but in the power of God.

1 Corinthians 2:6
Howbeit we speak wisdom among them that are perfect: yet not the wisdom of this world, nor of the princes of this world, that come to nought:

1 Corinthians 2:7
But we speak the wisdom of God in a mystery, even the hidden wisdom, which God ordained before the world unto our glory:

1 Corinthians 2:13
Which things also we speak, not in the words which man's wisdom teacheth, but which the Holy Ghost teacheth; comparing spiritual things with spiritual.

1 Corinthians 3:19
For the wisdom of this world is foolishness with God. For it is written, He taketh the wise in their own craftiness

1 Corinthians 1:30
But of him are ye in Christ Jesus, who of God is made unto us wisdom, and righteousness, and sanctification, and redemption:

1 Corinthians 1:17
For Christ sent me not to baptize, but to preach the gospel: not with wisdom of words, lest the cross of Christ should be made of none effect.

Luke 11:49
Therefore also said the wisdom of God, I will send them prophets and

apostles, and some of them they shall slay and persecute:

Luke 21:15

For I will give you a mouth and wisdom, which all your adversaries shall not be able to gainsay nor resist.

Acts 6:3

Wherefore, brethren, look ye out among you seven men of honest report, full of the Holy Ghost and wisdom, whom we may appoint over this business.

Acts 6:10

And they were not able to resist the wisdom and the spirit by which he spake.

The Spirit of Wisdom

Ephesians 1:17

That the God of our Lord Jesus Christ, the Father of glory, may give unto you the spirit of wisdom and revelation in the knowledge of him:

Ephesians 3:10

To the intent that now unto the principalities and powers in heavenly places might be known by the church the manifold wisdom of God,

1 Corinthians 12:8

For to one is given by the Spirit the word of wisdom; to another the word of knowledge by the same Spirit;

Proverbs 1:20

Wisdom crieth without; she uttereth her voice in the streets:

Proverbs 2:2

So that thou incline thine ear unto wisdom, and apply thine heart to understanding;

Proverbs 2:6

For the Lord giveth wisdom: out of his mouth cometh knowledge and understanding.

Proverbs 2:7

He layeth up sound wisdom for the righteous: he is a buckler to them that walk uprightly.

Proverbs 2:10

When wisdom entereth into thine heart, and knowledge is pleasant unto thy soul;

Proverbs 3:13

Happy is the man that findeth wisdom, and the man that getteth understanding.

Proverbs 3:19

The Lord by wisdom hath founded the earth; by understanding hath he established the heavens.

Proverbs 3:21

My son, let not them depart from thine eyes: keep sound wisdom and discretion:

Proverbs 4:5

Get wisdom, get understanding: forget it not; neither decline from the words of my mouth.

Proverbs 4:7

Wisdom is the principal thing; therefore get wisdom: and with all thy getting get understanding.

Proverbs 7:4

Say unto wisdom, Thou art my sister; and call understanding thy kinswoman:

Proverbs 8:1

Doth not wisdom cry? and understanding put forth her voice?

Proverbs 8:5

O ye simple, understand wisdom: and, ye fools, be ye of an understanding heart.

Proverbs 8:11

For wisdom is better than rubies; and all the things that may be desired are not to be compared to it.

Job 15:8

Hast thou heard the secret of God? and dost thou restrain wisdom to thyself?

Job 26:3

How hast thou counselled him that hath no wisdom? and how hast thou plentifully declared the thing as it is?

Job 28:12

But where shall wisdom be found? and where is the place of understanding?

Job 28:18

No mention shall be made of coral, or of pearls: for the price of wisdom is above rubies.

Job 28:20

Whence then cometh wisdom? and where is the place of understanding?

Prophetic Wisdom

Revelation 5:12

Saying with a loud voice, Worthy is the Lamb that was slain to receive power, and riches, and wisdom, and strength, and honour, and glory, and blessing.

Revelation 7:12

Saying, Amen: Blessing, and glory, and wisdom, and thanksgiving, and honour, and power, and might, be unto our God for ever and ever. Amen.

Revelation 13:18

Here is wisdom. Let him that hath understanding count the number of the beast: for it is the number of a man; and his number is Six hundred threescore and six.

Revelation 17:9

And here is the mind which hath wisdom. The seven heads are seven mountains, on which the woman sitteth.

Examples of Wisdom

(Paul)

2 Peter 3:15

And account that the longsuffering of our Lord is salvation; even as our beloved brother Paul also according to the wisdom given unto him hath written unto you;

(Daniel)

Daniel 5:14

I have even heard of thee, that the spirit of the gods is in thee, and that light and understanding and excellent wisdom is found in thee.

Daniel 1:17

As for these four children, God gave them knowledge and skill in all learning and wisdom: and Daniel had understanding in all visions and dreams.

(Moses)

And thou shalt speak unto all that are wise hearted, whom I have filled with the spirit of wisdom, that they may make Aaron's garments to consecrate him, that he may minister unto me in the priest's office.

Exodus 31:3

And I have filled him with the spirit of God, in wisdom, and in understanding, and in knowledge, and in all manner of workmanship,

Exodus 31:6

And I, behold, I have given with him Aholiab, the son of Ahisamach, of the tribe of Dan: and in the hearts of all that are wise hearted I have put wisdom, that they may make all that I have commanded thee;

Exodus 35:31

And he hath filled him with the spirit of God, in wisdom, in understanding, and in knowledge, and in all manner of workmanship;

Exodus 35:35

Them hath he filled with wisdom of heart, to work all manner of work, of the engraver, and of the cunning workman, and of the embroiderer, in blue, and in purple, in scarlet, and in fine linen, and of the weaver, even of them that do any work, and of those that devise cunning work.

Deuteronomy 4:6

Keep therefore and do them; for this is your wisdom and your understanding in the sight of the nations, which shall hear all these statutes, and say,

Surely this great nation is a wise and understanding people.

(Joshua)

Deuteronomy 34:9

And Joshua the son of Nun was full of the spirit of wisdom; for Moses had laid his hands upon him: and the children of Israel hearkened unto him, and did as the Lord commanded Moses.

(Daniel)

Daniel 1:20

And in all matters of wisdom and understanding, that the king enquired of them, he found them ten times better than all the magicians and astrologers that were in all his realm.

Daniel 2:14

Then Daniel answered with counsel and wisdom to Arioch the captain of the king's guard, which was gone forth to slay the wise men of Babylon:

Daniel 2:20

Daniel answered and said, Blessed be the name of God for ever and ever: for wisdom and might are his:

Daniel 2:21

And he changeth the times and the seasons: he removeth kings, and setteth up kings: he giveth wisdom unto the wise, and knowledge to them that know understanding:

Daniel 2:23

I thank thee, and praise thee, O thou God of my fathers, who hast given me wisdom and might, and hast made known unto me now what we desired of thee: for thou hast now made known unto us the king's matter.

Daniel 2:30

But as for me, this secret is not revealed to me for any wisdom that I have more than any living, but for their sakes that shall make known the interpretation to the king, and that thou mightest know the thoughts of thy heart.

Daniel 5:11

There is a man in thy kingdom, in whom is the spirit of the holy gods; and in the days of thy father light and understanding and wisdom, like the wisdom of the gods, was found in him; whom the king Nebuchadnezzar thy father, the king, I say, thy father, made master of the magicians, astrologers, Chaldeans, and soothsayers;

The Wisdom of Jesus

Micah 6:9

The Lord's voice crieth unto the city, and the man of wisdom shall see thy name: hear ye the rod, and who hath appointed it.

Matthew 11:19

The Son of man came eating and drinking, and they say, Behold a man gluttonous, and a winebibber, a friend of publicans and sinners. But wisdom is justified of her children.

Matthew 12:42

The queen of the south shall rise up in the judgment with this generation, and shall condemn it: for she came from the uttermost parts of the earth to hear the wisdom of Solomon; and, behold, a greater than Solomon is here.

Matthew 13:54

And when he was come into his own country, he taught them in their synagogue, insomuch that they were astonished, and said, Whence hath this man this wisdom, and these mighty works?

Mark 6:2

And when the sabbath day was come, he began to teach in the synagogue: and many hearing him were astonished, saying, From whence hath this man these things? and what wisdom is this which is given unto him, that even such mighty works are wrought by his hands?

Luke 1:17

And he shall go before him in the spirit and power of Elias, to turn the hearts of the fathers to the children, and the disobedient to the wisdom of the just; to make ready a people prepared for the Lord.

Luke 2:40

And the child grew, and waxed strong in spirit, filled with wisdom: and the grace of God was upon him.

Luke 2:52

And Jesus increased in wisdom and stature, and in favour with God and man.

Wise Nuggets

Proverbs 18:4

The words of a man's mouth are as deep waters, and the wellspring of wisdom as a flowing brook.

Proverbs 19:8

He that getteth wisdom loveth his own soul: he that keepeth understanding shall find good.

Proverbs 21:30

There is no wisdom nor understanding nor counsel against the Lord.

Proverbs 23:4

Labour not to be rich: cease from thine own wisdom.

Proverbs 23:9

Speak not in the ears of a fool: for he will despise the wisdom of thy words.

Proverbs 23:23

Buy the truth, and sell it not; also wisdom, and instruction, and understanding.

Proverbs 24:3

Through wisdom is an house builded; and by understanding it is established:

Proverbs 24:7

Wisdom is too high for a fool: he openeth not his mouth in the gate.

Proverbs 24:14

So shall the knowledge of wisdom be unto thy soul: when thou hast found it, then there shall be a reward, and thy expectation shall not be cut off.

Proverbs 29:3

Whoso loveth wisdom rejoiceth his father: but he that keepeth company with harlots spendeth his substance.

Family Wisdom

Proverbs 29:15

The rod and reproof give wisdom: but a child left to himself bringeth his mother to shame.

Proverbs 31:26

She openeth her mouth with wisdom; and in her tongue is the law of kindness.

Ecclesiastes 1:13

And I gave my heart to seek and search out by wisdom concerning all things that are done under heaven: this sore travail hath God given to the sons of man to be exercised therewith.

Proverbs 4:11

I have taught thee in the way of wisdom; I have led thee in right paths.

Solomon's Wisdom

Ecclesiastes 1:16

I communed with mine own heart, saying, Lo, I am come to great estate, and have gotten more wisdom than all they that have been before me in Jerusalem: yea, my heart had great experience of wisdom and knowledge.

Ecclesiastes 1:17

And I gave my heart to know wisdom, and to know madness and folly: I perceived that this also is vexation of spirit.

Ecclesiastes 1:18

For in much wisdom is much grief: and he that increaseth knowledge increaseth sorrow.

Ecclesiastes 2:3

I sought in mine heart to give myself unto wine, yet acquainting mine heart with wisdom; and to lay hold on folly, till I might see what was that good for the sons of men, which they should do under the heaven all the days of their life.

Ecclesiastes 2:9

So I was great, and increased more than all that were before me in Jerusalem: also my wisdom remained with me.

Ecclesiastes 2:12

And I turned myself to behold wisdom, and madness, and folly: for what can the man do that cometh after the king? even that which hath been already done.

Ecclesiastes 2:13

Then I saw that wisdom excelleth folly, as far as light excelleth darkness.

Financial Wisdom

Ecclesiastes 7:11

Wisdom is good with an inheritance: and by it there is profit to them that see the sun.

Ecclesiastes 7:12

For wisdom is a defence, and money is a defence: but the excellency of knowledge is, that wisdom giveth life to them that have it.

Ecclesiastes 7:19

Wisdom strengtheneth the wise more than ten mighty men which are in the city.

Ecclesiastes 7:23

All this have I proved by wisdom: I said, I will be wise; but it was far from me.

Ecclesiastes 7:25

I applied mine heart to know, and to search, and to seek out wisdom, and the reason of things, and to know the wickedness of folly, even of foolishness and madness:

Ecclesiastes 8:1

Who is as the wise man? and who knoweth the interpretation of a thing? a man's wisdom maketh his face to shine, and the boldness of his face shall be changed.

Ecclesiastes 8:16

When I applied mine heart to know wisdom, and to see the business that is done upon the earth: (for also there is that neither day nor night seeth sleep with his eyes:)

Ecclesiastes 9:10

Whatsoever thy hand findeth to do, do it with thy might; for there is no work, nor device, nor knowledge, nor wisdom, in the grave, whither thou goest.

Ecclesiastes 9:13

This wisdom have I seen also under the sun, and it seemed great unto me:

Ecclesiastes 9:15

Now there was found in it a poor wise man, and he by his wisdom delivered the city; yet no man remembered that same poor man.

Ecclesiastes 9:16

Then said I, Wisdom is better than strength: nevertheless the poor man's wisdom is despised, and his words are not heard.

Ecclesiastes 9:18

Wisdom is better than weapons of war: but one sinner destroyeth much good.

Ecclesiastes 10:1

Dead flies cause the ointment of the apothecary to send forth a stinking savour: so doth a little folly him that is in reputation for wisdom and honour.

Ecclesiastes 10:3

Yea also, when he that is a fool walketh by the way, his wisdom faileth him, and he saith to every one that he is a fool.

13

Understanding Scriptures

Proverbs 18:2 ESV

A fool takes no pleasure in understanding, but only in expressing his opinion.

Psalm 119:130 ESV

The unfolding of your words gives light; it imparts understanding to the simple.

Proverbs 14:29 ESV

Whoever is slow to anger has great understanding, but he who has a hasty temper exalts folly.

Proverbs 2:2-5 ESV

Making your ear attentive to wisdom and inclining your heart to understanding; yes, if you call out for insight and raise your voice for understanding, if you seek it like silver and search for it as for hidden treasures, then you will understand the fear of the Lord and find the knowledge of God.

Proverbs 17:27 ESV

Whoever restrains his words has knowledge, and he who has a cool spirit is a man of understanding.

Colossians 4:6 ESV

Let your speech always be gracious, seasoned with salt, so that you may know how you ought to answer each person.

Proverbs 3:13-18 ESV

Blessed is the one who finds wisdom, and the one who gets understanding, for the gain from her is better than gain from silver and her profit better than gold. She is more precious than jewels, and nothing you desire can compare with her. Long life is in her right hand; in her left hand are riches and honor. Her ways are ways of pleasantness, and all her paths are peace. …

Proverbs 4:7 ESV / 168

The beginning of wisdom is this: Get wisdom, and whatever you get, get insight.

Proverbs 12:1-28 ESV

Whoever loves discipline loves knowledge, but he who hates reproof is stupid. A good man obtains favor from the Lord, but a man of evil devices he condemns. No one is established by wickedness, but the root of the righteous will never be moved. An excellent wife is the crown of her husband, but she who brings shame is like rottenness in his bones. The thoughts of the righteous are just; the counsels of the wicked are deceitful. …

Proverbs 20:5 ESV

The purpose in a man's heart is like deep water, but a man of understanding will draw it our

2 Timothy 2:7 ESV

Think over what I say, for the Lord will give you understanding in everything.

Job 28:28 ESV

And he said to man, 'Behold, the fear of the Lord, that is wisdom, and to turn away from evil is understanding.'"

1 Corinthians 2:12 ESV

Now we have received not the spirit of the world, but the Spirit who is from God, that we might understand the things freely given us by God.

Proverbs 2:11-16 ESV

Discretion will watch over you, understanding will guard you, delivering you from the way of evil, from men of perverted speech, who forsake the paths of uprightness to walk in the ways of darkness, who rejoice in doing evil and delight in the perverseness of evil, men whose paths are crooked, and who are devious in their ways. …

Psalm 119:34 ESV / 58

Give me understanding, that I may keep your law and observe it with my whole heart.

Colossians 1:9-29 ESV

And so, from the day we heard, we have not ceased to pray for you, asking that you may be filled with the knowledge of his will in all spiritual wisdom and understanding, so as to walk in a manner worthy of the Lord, fully pleasing to him, bearing fruit in every good work and increasing in the knowledge of God. May you be strengthened with all power, according to his glorious might, for all endurance and patience with joy, giving thanks to the Father, who has qualified you to share in the inheritance of the saints in light. He has delivered us from the domain of darkness and transferred us to the kingdom of his beloved Son, …

Philippians 4:7 ESV

And the peace of God, which surpasses all understanding, will guard your hearts and your minds in Christ Jesus.

Psalm 111:10 ESV

The fear of the Lord is the beginning of wisdom; all those who practice it have a good understanding. His praise endures forever!

2 Timothy 3:16 ESV

All Scripture is breathed out by God and profitable for teaching, for reproof, for correction, and for training in righteousness,

Proverbs 3:5-6 ESV

Trust in the Lord with all your heart, and do not lean on your own understanding. In all your ways acknowledge him, and he will make straight your paths.

Proverbs 8:1 ESV

Does not wisdom call? Does not understanding raise her voice?

Proverbs 2:9 ESV / 33

Then you will understand righteousness and justice and equity, every good path;

Proverbs 1:7 ESV

The fear of the Lord is the beginning of knowledge; fools despise wisdom and instruction.

Acts 17:11 ESV / 31

Now these Jews were more noble than those in Thessalonica; they received the word with all eagerness, examining the Scriptures daily to see if these things were so.

Psalm 14:2-3 ESV / 30

The Lord looks down from heaven on the children of man, to see if there are any who understand, who seek after God. They have all turned aside; together they have become corrupt; there is none who does good, not even one.

John 16:13 ESV

When the Spirit of truth comes, he will guide you into all the truth, for he will not speak on his own authority, but whatever he hears he will speak, and he will declare to you the things that are to come.

James 3:17 ESV

But the wisdom from above is first pure, then peaceable, gentle, open to reason, full of mercy and good fruits, impartial and sincere.

1 Corinthians 2:13 ESV

And we impart this in words not taught by human wisdom but taught by the Spirit, interpreting spiritual truths to those who are spiritual.

2 Peter 3:16 ESV

As he does in all his letters when he speaks in them of these matters. There are some things in them that are hard to understand, which the ignorant and unstable twist to their own destruction, as they do the other Scriptures.

2 Timothy 2:15 ESV

Do your best to present yourself to God as one approved, a worker who has no need to be ashamed, rightly handling the word of truth.

Proverbs 2:6 ESV

For the Lord gives wisdom; from his mouth come knowledge and understanding;

Proverbs 9:10 ESV

The fear of the Lord is the beginning of wisdom, and the knowledge of the Holy One is insight.

2 Peter 3:18 ESV / 20 helpful votes

But grow in the grace and knowledge of our Lord and Savior Jesus Christ. To him be the glory both now and to the day of eternity. Amen.

Ephesians 1:17-19 ESV / 20 helpful votes

That the God of our Lord Jesus Christ, the Father of glory, may give you a spirit of wisdom and of revelation in the knowledge of him, having the eyes of your hearts enlightened, that you may know what is the hope to which he has called you, what are the riches of his glorious inheritance in the saints, and what is the immeasurable greatness of his power toward us who believe, according to the working of his great might

Proverbs 16:16 ESV

How much better to get wisdom than gold! To get understanding is to be chosen rather than silver.

John 14:26 ESV

But the Helper, the Holy Spirit, whom the Father will send in my name, he will teach you all things and bring to your remembrance all that I have said to you.

Ecclesiastes 7:12 ESV

For the protection of wisdom is like the protection of money, and the advantage of knowledge is that wisdom preserves the life of him who has it.

Matthew 13:23 ESV

As for what was sown on good soil, this is the one who hears the word and understands it. He indeed bears fruit and yields, in one case a hundredfold, in another sixty, and in another thirty."

Ecclesiastes 8:1 ESV

Who is like the wise? And who knows the interpretation of a thing? A man's wisdom makes his face shine, and the hardness of his face is changed.

Ephesians 1:17 ESV / 16

That the God of our Lord Jesus Christ, the Father of glory, may give you a spirit of wisdom and of revelation in the knowledge of him,

1 John 5:20 ESV

And we know that the Son of God has come and has given us understanding, so that we may know him who is true; and we are in him who is true, in his Son Jesus Christ. He is the true God and eternal life.

Jeremiah 29:11 ESV

For I know the plans I have for you, declares the Lord, plans for welfare and not for evil, to give you a future and a hope.

Psalm 119:18 ESV

Open my eyes, that I may behold wondrous things out of your law.

Hebrews 4:12 ESV

For the word of God is living and active, sharper than any two-edged sword, piercing to the division of soul and of spirit, of joints and of marrow, and discerning the thoughts and intentions of the heart.

Job 38:4 ESV

"Where were you when I laid the foundation of the earth? Tell me, if you have understanding.

Ephesians 1:18 ESV

Having the eyes of your hearts enlightened, that you may know what is the hope to which he has called you, what are the riches of his glorious inheritance in the saints,

Romans 11:33 ESV

Oh, the depth of the riches and wisdom and knowledge of God! How unsearchable are his judgments and how inscrutable his ways!

14

Faith Scriptures

Faith Scriptures

Matthew 8:26
   And he saith unto them, Why are ye fearful, O ye of little faith? Then he arose and rebuked the winds and the sea, and there was a great calm.

1 Thessalonians 3:10
   Night and day praying exceedingly that we might see your face, and might perfect that which is lacking in your faith

Colossians 2:7

Rooted and built up in him, and stablished in the faith, as ye have been taught, abounding therein with thanksgiving

Ephesians 3:12

[2] In whom we have boldness and access with confidence by the faith of him.

Ephesians 3:23

But before faith came, we were kept under the law, shut up unto the faith which should afterwards be revealed.

Ephesians 6:16

Above all, taking the shield of faith, wherewith ye shall be able to quench all the fiery darts of the wicked.

2 Corinthians 5:7

(For we walk by faith, not by sight:)

Romans 4:5

But to him that worketh not, but believeth on him that justifieth the ungodly, his faith is counted for righteousness

Romans 1:17

For therein is the righteousness of God revealed from faith to faith: as it is written, The just shall live by faith.

Romans 3:21-25

[22] Even the righteousness of God which is by faith of Jesus Christ unto all and upon all them that believe: for there is no difference:

[23] For all have sinned, and come short of the glory of God;

[24] Being justified freely by his grace through the redemption that is in Christ Jesus:

[25] Whom God hath set forth to be a propitiation through faith in his

blood, to declare his righteousness for the remission of past sins, through the forbearance of God;

Mark 11:22

And Jesus answering saith unto them, Have faith in God

<u>You can win!</u>

2 Thessalonians 5:8

But let us, who are of the day, be sober, putting on the breastplate of faith and love; and for an helmet, the hope of salvation.

Matthew 17:20

And Jesus said unto them, Because of your unbelief: for verily I say unto you, If ye have faith as a grain of mustard seed, ye shall say unto this mountain, Remove hence to yonder place; and it shall remove; and nothing shall be impossible unto you.

Acts 3:16

And his name through faith in his name hath made this man strong, whom ye see and know: yea, the faith which is by him hath given him this perfect soundness in the presence of you all.

Matthew 21:21

Luke 17:6

Jesus answered and said unto them, Verily I say unto you, If ye have faith, and doubt not, ye shall not only do this which is done to the fig tree, but also if ye shall say unto this mountain, Be thou removed, and be thou cast into the sea; it shall be done.

Galatians 2:16

Knowing that a man is not justified by the works of the law, but by the faith of Jesus Christ, even we have believed in Jesus Christ, that we might be justified by the faith of Christ, and not by the works of the law: for by the works of the law shall no flesh be justified·

Galatians 3:11

But that no man is justified by the law in the sight of God, it is evident: for, The just shall live by faith.

Romans 9:30

What shall we say then? That the Gentiles, which followed not after righteousness, have attained to righteousness, even the righteousness which is of faith

Your faith your victory. No faith no victory. It's just that simple. This seems overly simplified. It is not meant to be. Faith is a very complex topic that is based on the reading and integration of the Word of God. The more you look like the Word illustrated in John 1:1-5, the more faith you will have and the more victories you will have. The Bible laid out some formulas that are beneficial to learn.

Hope + Action = Faith
    (Hebrews 11:1)

Word of God+ Hearing+You= Faith (Romans 10:17)

Faith + you= The help of God
    (Mark 9:23)

You- Faith= No help from God
    (James 1:8)

Faith - Work= 0
    (James 2:26)

15

Coming Up

The Good Shepherd

The word pastor is derived from a Latin word meaning shepherd. The word shepherd means to move something from one place to another. The shepherd guides the sheep with love and attention. The pastor can wear all five-fold hats. Are you called to lead and guide? I hope you are. Pastors have been used by God to save and deliver souls from the hands of Satan.

We will discuss the five-fold mandate of the pastor. We will also review it's execution in modern times. Come join Zion Willingham as she reviews the call of the pastor, the Good Shepherd.

References

Newsmax website

Sermon Central

Piper, J. (2014). The marks of a spiritual leader.

Journey Online

OpenBible

Salvation

The Lord is not slack concerning his promise, as some men count slackness; but is longsuffering to us-ward, not willing that any should perish, but that all should come to repentance.

The most important act of faith is **salvation**. God does not want you to perish but he wants you to come into the salvation that was prepaid for you by Jesus Christ. If you know that you are unsaved, or you are unsure of the status of your salvation, today is the day of salvation.

John 3:16
  "For God so loved the world, as to give his only begotten Son; that whosoever believeth in him, may not perish, but may have life everlasting. ... For God so loved the world, that he gave his only Son, that whoever believes in him should not perish but have eternal life."

Romans 10:9-10
  That if thou shalt confess with thy mouth the Lord Jesus, and shalt believe in thine heart that God hath raised him from the dead, thou shalt be saved.

[10] For with the heart man believeth unto righteousness, and with the mouth, confession is made unto salvation.

So what will you do? It's yours if you will take it today. Do not make the mistake of listening to an evil spirit of procrastination about this matter.

2 Corinthians 6:2

*For he saith, I have heard thee in a time accepted, and in the day of salvation have I succoured thee: behold, **now** is the accepted time; behold, **now** is the day of salvation*

About the Author

Sanctuary Prayer Ministries is a ministry that exists with the sole purpose of seeking God in prayer, and fulfilling the great mandate.

Mark 16:15-16
  And he said unto them, Go ye into all the world, and preach the gospel to every creature.

He that believeth and is baptized shall be saved; but he that believeth not shall be damned.

We only have one agenda, and that Is to pray and study the Word of God.

Books written by Zion Willingham are available on all of the major ebook resellers.

Join our prayer service at https://www.spreaker.com/user/13834545

Also by Zion Willingham

Beautiful Feet

Are you called, chosen, or simply curious? The manifest series of books will explore each five-fold ministry call from biblical times until now. Beautiful Feet is the third title in the Manifest Series of books. We will discuss the evangelistic calling in its operation throughout the years. It's time to arise and manifest!

Come Out of the Cave

Are you called, chosen, or simply curious? The manifest series of books will explore each five-fold ministry call from biblical times until now. Come Out of the Cave is the second title in the Manifest Series of books. We will discuss the prophetic calling in its operation throughout the years. It's time to arise and manifest!

God's Spectacle

Are you called, chosen, or simply curious? The manifest series of books will explore each five-fold ministry call from biblical times until now. God's Spectacle is the first title in the Manifest Series of books. We will discuss the apostolic calling in its operation throughout the years. It's time to arise and manifest!

Not Quite Human

So what are we going to address in this book? We will find out what the Bible says, once and for all, about such controversial issues as aliens, astral realms, and the the authority of man.

Let's stop avoiding people who make claims about these things and search for the truth. I invite you to journey with me, as we explore those things that are not quite human

Self-Deliverance Manual

What do you do when you need freedom and there is no one available to help? What do you do when the amount of satanic concentration against your life is so thick that Pastors dare not help, for fear of the backlash? What do you do when the enemy has separated you from friends and family, and you can't find one person to agree with you? What do you do when your presence brings irritation and attacks to anyone you come into contact with? What do you do when unexplained demonic activities invade your home? The answer is simple, the method may not be. Deliverance is the answer. So what do you do when there is none to deliver? The good news is that Jesus Christ will deliver you.

The Holy Spirit brings about deliverance through yielded human beings. Therefore it stands to reason that if the extension cord is missing, you will need to plug yourself directly into the outlet of power. Will it be easy? It may or may not be easy. Deliverance can be compared to delivering a baby. It may be hard, long, and involve a lot of effort and pain, or it can be quick and easy. Either way, the results are worth the effort.

In his song, Hear the footsteps of Jesus, William J Kirkpatrick asked, Wilt thou be made whole" The question still lingers today. Do you hear Jesus calling you to be made whole?

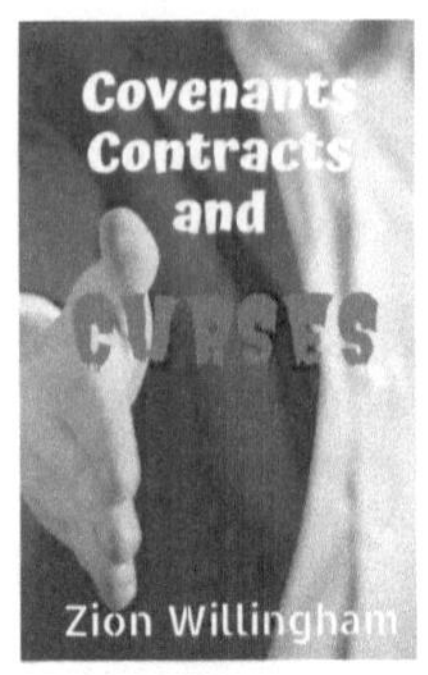

Covenants Contracts and Curses

Every fruit comes from a tree or vine. Every tree or vine comes from a root. Every root started as a seed. In order to chop down a massive tree one must cut down through the root and all seeds must be removed. Curses, Contracts, and Covenants work in the same fashion. This book will help you discern the seed of stubborn oppression, so that you can destroy the tree with its fruit

Mad As Hell

Hell is mad! To complete your victory, you must execute a madness that surpasses the madness of hell. If you are ready to complete your battle plan, you must exercise a greater level of madness than the powers that began the attack.

Zion Willingham explores an innovative new way to soak your home with prayers during sleep, and while you are away during the day. Use ingenuity to guard your home and perfect your victory in battle.

The final title in the Battle Plan Series will complete your battle with acidic renunciations, radical decrees and brutal pronouncements that are designed to be recorded, and played while you sleep. Read the rules of engagement to your environment, and that of your loved ones,